MECHIEL PUBLIS

10 TOP TIPS FOR BUSINESS SUCCESS

Jacqueline Brooks

Successful Entrepreneurs: 10 Top Tips for Business Success

First published in 2017

Copyright © Jacqueline Brooks 2017

All rights reserved. No part of this publication may be reproduced, stored in a retrieval system, or transmitted by any means, without the prior permission in writing from the publisher, nor be otherwise circulated in any form of binding or cover other than that in which it is published and with a similar condition including this condition being imposed on the subsequent purchaser.

Foreword

Nowadays the word **Entrepreneur** seems to be ringing out all around us. What does the word mean?
Entrepreneur = A person who sets up a business or businesses, taking on financial risks in the hope of profit. Or as Chris Oakley, chairman of web design company Chapter Eight puts it;

"An ***Entrepreneur*** sees an opportunity <u>which others do not fully recognise,</u> to meet an unsatisfied demand or to radically improve the performance of an existing business." Our role in this rapidly changing society is to be successful Entrepreneurs.

This book is a bitesize offering of the Top 10 Tips for **Business Success.** Keep it on your desk as an aide memoire for those of you setting up in business, both young and elderly, a book for all.

10 TOP TIPS FOR BUSINESS SUCCESS

"The wise man puts all his eggs in one basket... and watches the basket."
—Andrew Carnegie

Contents

Create Your Product: 1

When to Market your Product: 3

Use Marketing skills: 5

Create Opportunities: 7

Set up a System: 9

Find the Right Team: 11

How to make your Product stand out: 13

Contingency Plan: 15

Financial help: 17

The BIG secret ingredient: ..19

10 TOP TIPS FOR BUSINESS SUCCESS

10 TOP TIPS FOR BUSINESS SUCCESS

Create Your Product:

1. To succeed **CREATE** a product with the least product rejection.
   In other words, the product should be able to **SELL ITSELF.**

   Jot down your ideas on a notepad then put them in order of saleability.

   Think about what you can do to improve an existing product.

10 TOP TIPS FOR BUSINESS SUCCESS

"It always seems IMPOSSIBLE until it's done."

– Nelson Mandela

When to Market your Product:

2. Don't take a long time dithering to fine tune your product.
   SPEED TO MARKET is what you must aim for.
   Remember products are changing all the time and your product could become outdated the longer you spend fine tuning it.
   M.V.P = Minimum Viable Product.

| 10 TOP TIPS FOR BUSINESS SUCCESS

"If you can DREAM IT you can DO IT."

—Walt Disney

Use Marketing skills:

3. A valuable skill to have is **MARKETING SKILLS.** Understand your audience. Give them what they *WANT* and sell them what they *NEED.* Find out what they want and what they think could be better about your product idea.

    Use social media platforms to market your product.

    FACEBOOK Ads, Pinterest, Twitter and Instagram.

10 TOP TIPS FOR BUSINESS SUCCESS

"Have the COURAGE to follow your heart and intuition. They somehow know what you TRULY WANT TO BECOME."

—Steve Jobs

Create Opportunities:

4. Create **SALES OPPORTUNITIES**.
   Do you spend your time in long conversation with a potential customer? Do you forget one crucial element of sales?
   Ask yourself "why" people don't sell their products?
   Answer: "Always be closing a sale."
   Every opportunity to discuss
   your product, is an opportunity to sell your product.
   Be direct, **ask for the SALE!!**

| 10 TOP TIPS FOR BUSINESS SUCCESS

"Success consists of going from failure to failure without loss of ENTHUSIASM."

–Winston Churchill

Set up a System:

5. To be successful you should always run a **SIMPLE SYSTEM**.
Record everything you do, so you can teach your team.
It will be useful when you wish to have more quality time.
Check the system you have in place now. Is it simple?

What Most People Think

What Successful People Know

@douglaskarr

10 TOP TIPS FOR BUSINESS SUCCESS

"Entrepreneurs don't finish when **WE ARE TIRED** we finish when **WE ARE DONE.**"

—Robert Kiyosa

Find the Right Team:

6. You need the right team to work with – **TALENT FUNNEL** – constantly be looking for staff with the right attitude, not just the right skills. (This will be most beneficial when your business decides to Scale Up.)

10 TOP TIPS FOR BUSINESS SUCCESS

"The *SECRET* of BUSINESS is to know something that nobody else knows."

–Aristotle Onassis

How to make your Product stand out:

7. One important building block to your business success is a **STRONG BRAND.**
   You should create two brands.
   Create a physical brand and a social brand online. Have an appealing logo.
   Your brand represents your company image on the global stage.
   Give it thought, time and energy.

| 10 TOP TIPS FOR BUSINESS SUCCESS

"Dreamers and Doers are not two different people. All the BEST ENTREPRENEURS are a bit of both."

–Mandy McEwan

Contingency Plan:

8. You have heard the phrase "Never put all your eggs in one basket;" Well, there has to be **DIVERSITY IN BUSINESS**. If your business is just in the property market, what contingency do you have if there is a property crash? Have a mixture of investments, like technology, retail, etc...

Teamwork

coming together is a beginning
keeping together is a process
working together is success

-Henry Ford

10 TOP TIPS FOR BUSINESS SUCCESS

"THE BIGGEST RISK IS NOT TAKING ANY RISK. IN A WORLD THAT'S CHANGING REALLY QUICKLY, THE ONLY STRATEGY THAT IS GUARANTEED TO FAIL IS NOT TAKING RISKS."

~MARK ZUCKERBERG

Financial help:

9. **RAISING FINANCE** – allow the business to grow. Make sure you get the business model right to get financial backers.

| 10 TOP TIPS FOR BUSINESS SUCCESS

"I am THANKFUL to those who said NO to me. It's because of them.... I DID IT MYSELF."

– Albert Einstein

The BIG secret ingredient:

10. Every business must be…**RECURRING** or your business will go bust!!!! If people buy into your business how will ensure repeat sales?? If you have 100 people paying £100 per month, you will have to continue to delivery products that meet their needs, to maintain that level of profit.

Wishing you every success in your business.

Jacqueline Brooks

10 TOP TIPS FOR BUSINESS SUCCESS

p.s. If you have found this information useful please send me an email:

post.ed@hotmail.co.uk

Printed in Great Britain
by Amazon